PROSPECTS FOR PEACE IN THE MIDDLE EAST

Joseph J. Sisco, *Moderator*

George Ball
J. William Fulbright
Rita Hauser
Jacob Javits

A Round Table held on September 26, 1977
and sponsored by
the American Enterprise Institute for Public Policy Research
Washington, D.C.

This pamphlet contains the edited transcript of
one of a series of AEI forums.
These forums offer a medium for
informal exchanges of ideas on current policy problems
of national and international import.
As part of AEI's program for providing opportunities
for the presentation of competing views,
they serve to enhance the prospect
that decisions within our democracy will be based
on a more informed public opinion.
AEI forums are also available on
audio and color-video cassettes.

AEI Forum 11

Printed in United States of America

Library of Congress Cataloging in Publication Data

Sisco, Joseph J.
"Prospects for peace in the Middle East", Monday, September 26, 1977.
   (AEI forum ; no. 11)
   1. Jewish-Arab relation—1973–   —Congresses. I. Javits, Jacob Kop-
pel, 1904–   II. American Enterprise Institute for Public Policy Re-
search. III. Title. IV. Title: Prospects for peace in the Middle East. V. Series:
American Enterprise Institute for Public Policy Research. AEI public policy
forum ; no. 11.
DS119.7.S55   327.5694′017′4927   77-17276
ISBN 0-8447-2110-7

JOSEPH SISCO, president of the American University and forum moderator: I see many, many friends in the audience, and I want to say to my panelists that we are among experts. I feel a little bit like the man who could talk about nothing other than how he survived the great Johnstown flood of the 1930s. Everywhere he went the only thing he talked about was how he survived the Johnstown flood. When he died and went up through the pearly gates, Saint Peter welcomed him and said, "What would you like to do today? You have a very easy day: a tea at four o'clock, and, of course, you'll be expected to make some appropriate remarks."

And the man said, "Fine, I'd like to talk about how I survived the Johnstown flood."

Saint Peter delayed a bit and said, "Well, all right, if you insist. But will you bear one thing in mind?"

And the man said, "What's that?"

"Noah will be in the audience."

[Laughter.]

Now, panelists, I want you to bear in mind that we are among experts.

The history of the Middle East has been a history of lost opportunities and the year 1977 has been characterized as a year of opportunity. Is it to be lost, and is the area to return to the vortex of violence and counterviolence that has been so characteristic of it over the years?

1

There are both positive and negative factors in the situation. The balance of military strength in the area is a logical deterrent to war, but logic has not always prevailed in the Middle East. Peoples on both sides of the conflict are absolutely sick and tired of war. They are ready to support another peaceful effort.

Israel continues to question whether the Arabs want real peace and coexistence or merely a tactical hiatus during which another war can be launched, aimed at its extinction. And the Arabs hold a deeply rooted fear that Israel favors territory over peace, a fear reinforced by the policies of the new Israeli leadership.

Yet, both sides have experienced successful negotiations. Both are satisfied with the three interim agreements that were achieved in recent years. Moreover, an international framework for negotiations exists. In November 1967, the UN Security Council adopted Resolution 242, which contains the principal elements of peace. It calls for withdrawal of Israeli forces from territory occupied in the 1967 war, cessation of all forms of belligerency, freedom of navigation through the Suez Canal and other waterways, settlement of the Palestine refugee problem, and territorial inviolability and political independence of every state in the area—including Israel. Still, the chasm of distrust remains very deep indeed.

Senator Jacob Javits is the ranking member of the Senate Foreign Relations Committee. In 1970 he was a delegate to the twenty-fifth General Assembly of the United Nations. Senator Javits, how do you see the prospects in the area at the present time?

JACOB JAVITS, United States senator (Republican, New York): I think the prospects have improved lately, for two reasons. First, the Begin government can deliver—and this has been a problem with Israel for some time. Mr. Begin seems to have established a position which will enable him to get a peace agreement approved by the people of Israel and by the Israeli parliament, the Knesset.

Second, I find in the Middle East an overwhelming combination of deep war-weariness, particularly in Egypt, and grave economic difficulty, which should be a very powerful inducement to peace.

I do not believe that peace will be accomplished in one fell swoop or by some package that will be wrapped up and delivered by President Carter or anybody else, but I think we have a pretty good chance now of seeing the start of a process which will lead to a stabilization of the situation. In short, I do believe that the prospects are better than I have seen in a long while.

MR. SISCO: Mr. J. William Fulbright served one term in the House of Representatives and thirty years in the Senate before leaving that body in December 1974. While in the Senate, Mr. Fulbright distinguished himself as the chairman of the Committee on Foreign Relations for some fifteen years. Senator Fulbright also contributed to the advancement of scholarship through the Fulbright-Hays Fellowship Program.

J. WILLIAM FULBRIGHT, former member of the United States Senate (Democrat, Arkansas): The Middle East is the most difficult of all foreign policy issues to discuss objectively, candidly, and without rancor, in public forums. The deep and powerful emotions inherent in this issue find few, if any, parallels in our history.

As a member of the Foreign Relations Committee of the Senate, I was concerned with this subject for twenty-five years. At present, the firm of Hogan and Hartson, of which I am a member, is registered as a legal representative of the governments of Saudi Arabia and the United Arab Emirates, but the views I express long antedate that connection. They are spoken not in my professional capacity as a lawyer, but simply as an American citizen, concerned primarily with the best interests of the United States.

The Arab-Israeli conflict is a dangerous threat to peace and to our national interests. It also provides a great opportunity for constructive statesmanship. Historical events, beyond our control, have resulted in the United States being the decisive factor either in achieving a solution of the conflict or in perpetuating it. Our role in this matter is fraught with the most serious consequences for good or evil for all of us.

I am concerned that an unprecedented, and possibly irretrievable, opportunity for peace is slipping through our hands. On the one side, the principal Arab nations have unified their policies and become willing to accept a settlement under which Israel would be assured a reasonably secure national existence. On the other side, the Begin government, highly nationalistic and motivated by ancient historical claims as well as by considerations of national security, is pursuing a policy that offers little promise of an early general settlement.

Prime Minister Begin is able to sustain this policy only because the United States continues to provide the indispensable economic and military means to do so, even though this enables Israel to resist and, at times, defeat the objectives of the United States. The preservation of the integrity of Israel is, of course, one objective of our national policy, but it is not the only interest we have in the Middle East. It is the responsibility of President Carter to reconcile the various objectives and not to give Israel's defense an absolute priority that jeopardizes all other interests.

Some of our other objectives are: to minimize or eliminate the Middle East as a source of confrontation with the Soviet Union; to ensure continued access to the energy resources of the Persian Gulf states, which are essential to

4

the economic health of the United States, Europe, and Japan; and to uphold the principles of the United Nations Charter, and the principles spelled out in UN Security Council Resolution 242 of November 1967 pertaining to the Middle East.

The essential elements of a reasonable peace settlement are now well known and widely agreed upon by reasonable people of diverse personal sympathies. These terms were skillfully codified in 1975 by a Brookings Institution study group, on which Rita Hauser served, and that group's recommendations have received wide approval. Another member of tonight's panel, Mr. George Ball, has an article in the April issue of *Foreign Affairs* which also presents a thoughtful and perceptive discussion of the subject. No further studies are needed to ascertain the reasonable terms of peace. The challenge now is to act upon our own stated objectives.

By general agreement, Israel today has clear military superiority in the area, so the former plea that it could make no concessions when weak no longer applies. The premise that military superiority would make Israel flexible has been tested and found wanting. The only other incentive the United States can apply is to limit and, if necessary, reduce our military and economic support.

This issue poses a challenge of the highest consequence to our national leadership. The question upon which war or peace depends is whether the President of the United States can muster the strength and determination to pursue a policy that is both equitable to the parties in the Middle East and solidly based upon the national interests of the United States.

MR. SISCO: Mr. George Ball is the senior partner with Lehman Brothers in New York. He was under secretary of state in the Kennedy and Johnson administrations, and served as the U.S. ambassador to the United Nations in 1968.

GEORGE BALL, former under secretary of state: Obviously, the national interest of the United States is to avoid war in the Middle East. Nothing would be more destructive than another war and the oil embargo that would inevitably accompany it. The new kind of war, with surface-to-surface missiles, would be highly destructive; it would engage the fate of the civilian populations on both sides. From the point of view of a larger world struggle, it would present the very serious danger of a superpower confrontation. Finally, the oil embargo, if invoked again, would disrupt the unity of the non-Communist world with costs that are incalculable.

How do we bring about peace? What is involved? The basic outlines of a settlement have been known ever since Resolution 242 was adopted in 1967 by the Security Council of the United Nations.

From the point of view of the United States, a real peace, not merely a declaration of nonbelligerency, is required. And I think that the government of Israel is quite right in insisting that there be a real peace. But to have a real peace, there must also be a withdrawal by Israel from the territories taken in 1967—a substantial, if not complete, withdrawal, in which the areas for discussion are limited.

There must also be some provision made for a homeland for the Palestinians. The situation that has prevailed for ten years is intolerable. The United States should not move toward subsidizing a military occupation of more than a million people on the West Bank or on the Gaza Strip who have been denied suffrage and an opportunity for self-determination. We have to face this issue squarely and insist upon a Palestinian homeland. As Senator Fulbright suggested, we have the means to insist upon it, if we will.

These are the elements which seem essential to a settlement and which will be a great test of the strength and determination that underlie U.S. foreign policy. It will be a great test of the President's determination as well, for if he lacks the will to see this through, the future could be very, very dubious.

If the conference breaks down or if no conference can be held, the Arab nations will almost certainly seek a military solution, for which they can arm themselves within two or three years; and they have the wealth to do it. This will lead to incalculable consequences to our national interest.

MR. SISCO: Rita Hauser, an international lawyer with the firm of Stroock and Stroock and Lavan in New York, was a member of the Brookings Institution study group on the Middle East. She has served as U.S. representative to the United Nations Commission on Human Rights and as a member of the U.S. delegation to the United Nations General Assembly. Mrs. Hauser, I hope that you will address yourself to a question which was raised directly or indirectly by both Mr. Fulbright and George Ball; does U.S. support of Israel adversely affect our other interests in the area? And how would you define those interests?

RITA HAUSER, attorney and former member of the Brookings Institution study group on the Middle East: I think the situation is extremely propitious for peace in the Middle East for two fundamental reasons: first, this administration, like the preceding one, understands the need for America to act as a dynamic catalyst in bringing both sides to the bargaining table. Both administrations, particularly the current one, have seemed willing to do that.

Second, Russian interests seem to coincide with our own. At least for the moment, all indications are that they would cooperate in a peace endeavor and would not impede it.

If the United States understands that both patience and care are required in getting these parties to the bargaining table—and if we do not attempt to impose our own solutions, but limit ourselves to gently easing the parties to the conference table, I believe, as Senator Javits does, that both sides will want to bargain and to negotiate a peace, the contours of which are fairly clear. It is our role to encourage not only Israel, but also the Arab nations, to go to the conference table. And, at the moment, the single impediment in getting them there is the problem of representation of the Palestine Liberation Organization. I hope very much that the administration will not succumb to the easy prospect of trying to get the PLO to modify its stand in some ambiguous way, and then urge Israel to compromise with the PLO. In my view, that effort will fail. It will cause great bitterness and may, in itself, defeat the conference.

If the administration exercises care in meeting with both sides, we can get them to the conference table. It is in our interest to get them there and to begin the negotiations, which may take a very long time.

The Brookings report to which I contributed envisaged a peace process that might span ten to twenty years. In place of war, a normalization process would begin, involving trade, cultural exchange, building for the next generation, and, ultimately, peace.

Mr. Sisco: I think this panel is all agreed that there is an unusual opportunity this year. Each of the panelists has indicated that the U.S. role is an important one, though there may be differences of view as to what that role might be.

Mr. Fulbright and Senator Javits raised the issue of American support of Israel. Where does that fit into our overall interests? Does the support of Israel jeopardize our other interests?

SENATOR JAVITS: Senator Fulbright and I have differed on that for almost all the twenty-five years he has been talking about it, and, so far, time has been on my side. The fact is, U.S. interests have not been compromised. We have more influence in the Middle East than we ever had before, and the Soviet Union is pretty well counted out in terms of its ability to bring about a peace. And yet, the constant cry for twenty-five years has been to force Israel into making peace. Twenty-five years of experience belies that policy, notwithstanding the four wars which were engendered to keep this little nation alive.

Mr. Ball and Senator Fulbright disregard the fundamental fact that Israel doesn't even have to lose a war to cease to exist—it only has to lose one battle and it is finished.

The Arab states have enormous resources. Mr. Ball just said that they have all the money in the world. As a matter of fact, Egypt is in very serious economic straits, notwithstanding all the money that Saudia Arabia and Kuwait might have. But be that as it may, these *force majeure* tactics will bring about neither a peace nor a stabilization of the area, nor will they safeguard our interest in bringing the area into some kind of modern living condition.

The example of democracy provided by Israel is beginning to have a positive effect throughout the Arab world. Mr. Ball said the Palestinians have had no suffrage. On the West Bank elections were held recently that were certified by everyone, including the enemies of Israel, as being completely democratic, notwithstanding the fact that most of the mayors are pro-PLO. Honest elections in the Middle East are unheard of, and yet that is what has happened on the West Bank.

This process has to be given a chance. The way to do this is to keep the parties' feet to the fire. But the minute we threaten to cut off military support from Israel, leaving it at the mercy of the worst elements in the Arab world, we will bring on war by giving the Arabs the illusion that the United States will deliver to them what they have not been able to gain for themselves in four wars.

MR. BALL: I would like to clarify my position on one matter. I am all for the support of Israel. The United States should continue to lend its full support to Israel. The question for the United States is not whether we support Israel, but what kind of situation we are prepared to subsidize. This is a matter of American national interest. It is a decision that cannot be made in Jerusalem; it has to be made in Washington.

What kind of situation are we prepared to subsidize? Certainly not a situation of stalemate that can lead to disaster. We should, by all means, use what elements of persuasion we have in order to try to bring about a peace which we regard as fair and reasonable, and which meets the legitimate interests of all sides.

Concerning the issue of suffrage, I would like to ask Senator Javits if he thinks the people of New York would have full suffrage if they were entitled to vote for the mayor of New York but not for the distinguished senator from New York. This is the situation that now prevails in the West Bank—the people can vote in local elections, but they cannot vote on anything that affects the whole area.

SENATOR JAVITS: The West Bank has never had even this much suffrage before, or this much democracy. When the British abandoned it, it became *terra franca,* free territory for anybody to take, and Jordan took it. That is the only reason why Jordan ever possessed it, or why we have an argument about whether it is occupied territory. Under what mandate did Jordan occupy it?

In view of the history of the people on the West Bank, your statement that they have no suffrage is simply untrue.

10

They have unique suffrage, and they are enjoying the benefits of it now.

It is true that they do not elect senators. There is no national legislature to elect them to.

MR. BALL: My point is that the Palestinians will be denied any possibility of self-determination as long as the present situation continues. In effect, they are under the colonial and military domination of Israel. This has gone on for ten years, and that is long enough. Colonialism of the kind we see here is an anachronism. I cannot imagine that you would defend colonialism.

SENATOR JAVITS: But, Mr. Ball, I don't hear any proposition from you for a period of trusteeship and tutelage that would give political parties a chance to get going on the West Bank, and would prevent the 30,000 PLO riflemen, now shooting their way through southern Lebanon, from descending into the West Bank and making it a comparable battleground. Israel has not argued against giving these people an opportunity to find their own way and to have an opportunity for self-determination. I'm not drawing up any briefs for the government of Israel. All I say is that your *force majeure* may well force the West Bank to become another Lebanon.

MR. BALL: I think it is odd to speak out against force when we are talking about military occupation to start with.

MRS. HAUSER: I think it is fair to ask why the occupation has endured as long as ten years.

After Israel won a decisive victory in 1967, everyone, including Israel, expected an immediate turn to the conference table, which is normal after war and victory. But six months later, at Khartoum, the Arab countries issued their famous "three noes": they would not negotiate, they would

11

not recognize Israel, and they would not sign a peace treaty.

The consequence is that an occupation has endured which is not what Israel expected and probably not what most Israelis would like to see continued. Throughout, the problem has been that the Arabs refused to accept the existence of Israel; they have done this on every occasion. And we have come to the point where they have exhausted themselves. They know they cannot win on the battlefield, so they are trying to get to a Geneva conference. Yet, they still persist in dragging up this red herring, the PLO, which is, in my view, a greater problem for the Arabs than for Israel.

Take the example of Lebanon, which has been dismembered. Lebanon was a "Christian-dominated" country with a problem of adequate Moslem representation. Basically the Christians were attacked by the PLO interests, and everywhere the PLO exercises its control, there is disorder. And, yet, the Arabs continue to press the PLO cause. For many people this is a signal that they are not yet serious about peace, that they are not serious about recognizing the state of Israel. Once the Arabs have come to accept the fact that Israel exists, peace can readily be achieved. I know of no issue that would come before the Geneva conference on which a compromise solution could not be found without too much difficulty.

MR. BALL: I think that the responsible Arab states are prepared to compromise, though they may not, at this point, want to give away their total bargaining position, any more than the Israelis do.

I don't want to appear to defend the Arab side against the Israeli side, but I want to point out that the United States has a national interest which we have to assert, and that we have to make up our mind what kind of situation we will support. This is a part of our responsibility.

MR. SISCO: Two kinds of questions are faced this year, one procedural, and one of a substantive nature. On the procedural side, the key question is: Should there be Palestinian representation at a renewed Geneva conference? The Israeli position is that it will not sit down with the PLO. Yet, some proposals have been put forward by the Israeli government that would affect Palestinians from the West Bank. What about this issue of Palestinian representation at Geneva?

MR. FULBRIGHT: I wonder if I could say a word. I am still on the panel. [Laughter.]

MR. SISCO: You have been very quiet, Bill.

MR. FULBRIGHT: Well, I didn't wish to intervene in the dialogue that was going on here.

There are two or three things that I certainly don't agree to. Concerning this business of *force majeure,* I am certainly not suggesting that we force Israel to do anything, just that we stop subsidizing their occupation and their war-making capacity.

The Israelis can make war because we furnish them the means to do so. They expect us to continue to support their occupation. If they should start a new, preemptive war, they would expect us to support that.

There is a danger that they will start another war which will create a great emotional outcry and pose problems for our President that will have repercussions upon this entire country.

No one is suggesting, in either the Brookings report or Mr. Ball's article, that we abandon Israel. I said, as long ago as 1970, that I was willing to support a bilateral guarantee of the integrity of both Israel and the Arab states in the area. The UN Security Council ought to see to this. It has the

13

precedent of the tripartite declaration of 1950. No one is saying that we should leave anyone to the mercy of anyone else. We must try to stabilize the area. I would be more than willing to enter into agreements with both sides in conjunction with the UN Security Council.

Israel is very powerful militarily, because we have given it far more and better weapons than are possessed by all the Arab states together. The military situation is quite satisfactory from the Israeli point of view, and, of course, that gives them no incentive to do anything.

It is not particularly relevant to the national interest of the United States whether suffrage on the West Bank is full or only partial. It is in the interest of the United States, as we said in the beginning, to avoid a war, to bring about peace. And that is also in the interest of Israel.

Mr. Ball's article, "How to Save Israel in Spite of Herself," is germane to my point. It is not uncommon for an elected official, who thinks it is in the interest of his country to make a certain unpalatable decision, to blame someone else for that decision. The United States, because of its history and its position, ought to take that blame. It is in our national interest to relieve the government of Israel from making the unpalatable decision of sitting down with the PLO.

The PLO is simply a symbol. It is the more current symbol of the terrorism which Mr. Begin, himself, originated a few years ago, long before the PLO was known. This terrorism grows naturally out of the kind of situation that has arisen there and in other parts of the world.

Again, it is in the interest of the United States to settle that issue, and, if it involves withdrawing military support, then that is what must be done.

SENATOR JAVITS: That is a real echo of the past, without any regard for the present. For one thing, the PLO has demonstrated in Lebanon what it really is—an extremely destructive force—not just revolutionary but really anarchic. It cannot even cooperate with Syria, one of the confrontation Arab states. With 30,000 troops in Lebanon, Syria cannot prevent the PLO from waging a war against the Christian Lebanese.

MR. FULBRIGHT: I don't defend the violence of the PLO, but to get a conference going that could educate the PLO, that could change it from the kind of organization it is, would be in the interest of Israel as well as the United States. Right now, we have a stalemate.

As long ago as 1975, these same sentiments were expressed, but Mr. Kissinger gave up all his efforts, and said the intransigence of the Israeli government was too great, and that we would have to reassess our policy. Of course, he didn't do that because the Congress would not let him. So we ended up with piecemeal negotiations, which have been of little value. And at the time, I made a speech to that effect to the Middle East Institute annual meeting, but that is history.

What do we do now, under these circumstances? This is a time of opportunity which we must seize, as we cannot expect this situation to stay the same indefinitely. Something is bound to give, and that something won't be good unless there is some progress.

I agree with Mrs. Hauser that it will not be done neatly, in one package, and that we must require the Arab leaders to do what they have said they would. It would take some time, but we would be moving in the right direction. There is no movement now that I can see, none at all. The recent reaction of Mr. Begin to President Carter's very polite reception was to go back home and start two more Israeli settlements on the West Bank. It looked as if he was showing that he really doesn't even have to bother about President Carter. And shortly thereafter, General Allon said 2 million Israelis might move into the West Bank, which was directly contrary to what Mr. Carter had said was our policy. If that is not blatant defiance of the U.S. government, I don't know what is. To continue to subsidize it, it seems to me, is most unusual in the history of modern political life. [Laughter].

MRS. HAUSER: But it seems to me, Mr. Fulbright, you had a long experience with subsidizing a government that defied us quite frequently, and we got into a war about it, didn't we? So far, by supporting Israel, we have managed to keep ourselves effectively out of conflict.

MR. FULBRIGHT: Who are you talking about?

MRS. HAUSER: I was thinking about Vietnam, but we won't introduce that subject this evening.

MR. FULBRIGHT: Oh, dear me. [Laughter.]

MRS. HAUSER: By subsidizing Israel, the United States is—

MR. FULBRIGHT: Do you think we'll get in the same situation?

MRS. HAUSER: No, on the contrary. [Laughter.]

By supporting a strong Israel, we have been able to keep ourselves out of the area. We have a strong ally in Israel, and it has been one of the effective pins of our military policy in the region. In addition, we have a historic moral commitment to Israel.

It is most important for all of us to try to understand that our government, by giving or withholding military support, will not affect the outcome in the area. That is a myth which many people believe. The countries of the Middle East have wills of their own, and they will use every method at their disposal to carry out their policies. We have seen Egypt, for example, a minion of Russia, drop Russia and come to the United States. Egypt plays the game as it sees fit, and so does Israel.

We should not press, force, or otherwise induce them to accept a settlement preconceived by the United States. Instead, we should take the harder but more modest task of trying to induce them to come to a conference table.

We will not induce Israel to a conference table by cutting off its military assistance. We will not get a peace settlement in this country by doing a "reassessment."

I don't have to speak for the Senate since Senator Javits is here, but I would say that the previous reassessment failed because the American people did not support it.

SENATOR JAVITS: The reassessment resulted in a historic move toward peace—the second Sinai agreement actually restored major areas of the Sinai, including the oilfields, to Egypt. One cannot just dismiss the process as hopeless and bankrupt. It worked in that particular instance, and it worked before in the agreements with Syria and Egypt in 1974.

We seem to be talking about a dream world. The Israeli cabinet has now decided that it will go to Geneva with a unified Arab delegation, even if that delegation has strong PLO sympathizers. But Israel will not accept representatives of the PLO because the PLO, notwithstanding all its blandishments of getting along well with the United States and its Arab brothers, still wants, as part of its fundamental constitution, to liquidate Israel. How on earth can we ask a nation to negotiate with an entity that wills its destruction?

MR. BALL: Of course, this is what negotiation is all about. After every war the customary—

SENATOR JAVITS: But this is during the war, George, not after. The PLO wills Israel's destruction now. There is no "after."

MR. BALL: In every peace conference with contending factions, each faction would probably like to see the other destroyed. This has been the case in almost every historic situation.

I see no real reason why these parties should not negotiate. We are interested in what comes out, not what goes in; this is the important factor.

My question is, Are we going to accomplish anything by getting the parties to a Geneva conference? At present they are so far apart in their stated positions that, unless we can begin to bring them closer together, a Geneva conference could be a very dangerous, high-risk enterprise.

MR. FULBRIGHT: Failure would be a disaster.

SENATOR JAVITS: It is amazing that this peace conference is what Mr. Ball wants more than anything else, and yet he does not want it. This is fantastic. He wants a peace conference, and he wants the Israelis there, but he wants peace on terms he writes. They may not be the right terms, even for our country.

MR. BALL: Senator, I don't want a peace conference, I want peace. I think they may be quite distinct things, judging from the history of peace conferences. Unless a good deal of preliminary work has been done, and unless the parties are moving toward one another, a peace conference could be a disaster.

We certainly ought to keep pressing for a conference but, more importantly, we ought to try at the same time to get the parties to come to grips with each other on the fundamental issues.

MR. SISCO: Well, the Carter administration is moving forward on both fronts—the procedural issue of Palestinian representation and the substantive issue of a final settlement.

MR. BALL: You don't have to defend this administration. You are not in it.

SENATOR JAVITS: And if I may say so, look what a shambles was made of Carter's effort to lay it all out on the table, with everybody making concessions, so that all we would need to do is go to Geneva to have it blessed.

President Carter tried exactly that earlier this year, and all it accomplished was to feed Arab illusions and Israeli fears. It could not have been a worse defeat.

The Israelis have undertaken to negotiate anything— settlements, occupied areas or administered areas. They have said they are willing to negotiate every particular issue. Therefore, the United States should bring them to Geneva and do its utmost as a mediator to negotiate a deal. I believe it can be done.

Why say that it cannot be done without an advance agreement? We have never been able to get one, and if we try again, it could be a disaster.

MR. BALL: Unless both parties are moving in the same direction, a peace conference can become very dangerous. It can be the occasion for a dramatic restatement of hard positions by each side and an ultimate breakdown of communication, which would be disastrous.

I am suggesting only that we need to work very hard, and, by the way, I think that what President Carter has done so far is splendid. I disagree with you, Senator Javits, when you suggest that it has been counterproductive. As a result of the U.S. effort to put forward the outlines of a position, we are closer to getting somewhere than we have been for a very long time.

Mr. Fulbright: The senator from New York stated that the Israelis are willing to negotiate. Nearly everything that has taken place since Mr. Begin's visit would indicate that they have no intention of giving up any territory, and what they have done in the West Bank indicates that they have no intention whatever of giving it up. No country that intends to give up territory would continue to make settlements and spend a great deal of money in the process. Think of the extreme statement of General Allon about moving 2 million people to the West Bank. And the other day the President said something about the PLO which Rabbi Sternstein characterized as an attack similar to that of the Arabs at the Yom Kippur War. This is a very provocative statement, it seems to me.

I see no indication of a conciliatory attitude even toward the United States, much less the PLO, on the part of spokesmen of the government of Israel recently, especially since Mr. Begin's visit.

Senator Javits: The fundamental conciliation has just taken place—the agreement to go to Geneva with a unified Arab delegation and start the negotiations for peace, with no holds barred. The negotiations, Senator Fulbright, will include the Israeli settlements on the West Bank. When I came back from Israel about a year ago, I said that when the Israelis establish a settlement in a territory, that does not mean that juridically they will keep it. With all respect, I think what I had to say is at least to be equated with Rabbi Sternstein. A thousand Arab muftis have probably made much bloodier vows than Rabbi Sternstein.

Mrs. Hauser: But let's come back to the fundamentals Joe Sisco pointed out. We have the contour for peace in Resolution 242, which calls for secure and recognized boundaries to be negotiated by the parties among themselves.

Why have we drifted away from that fundamental bedrock of our policy? The Israelis resist going to a Geneva conference with the PLO not because of their distaste for dealing with a terrorist organization, but because the PLO wants representation qua PLO—a predetermination that the conference will accord them something, such as a Palestinian state, which they would presumably dominate.

That is something Israel is unwilling to accept, and I think rightly, because it would fundamentally destabilize the Middle East, as the conflict in Lebanon has shown.

Why people have tended to disregard this brutal, bloody, destructive conflict—who caused it, and what the forces at play are—mystifies me.

We tend to ignore the destructive role of the PLO in that conflict and continue to say that the PLO must have a place in making peace in the area.

The Israelis resist going to the conference table because of the PLO. I think they are right, and I think the American people stand behind that proposition.

MR. FULBRIGHT: It's not at all clear that blame for Lebanon entirely belongs with the PLO. The Israelis have been shelling it and have positions in it and so on. It is very unclear just who is responsible for that part of it.

MRS. HAUSER: That's not how the war started, Senator Fulbright.

SENATOR JAVITS: That's not how it's being fought.

MR. FULBRIGHT: From the Israelis' point of view, this is not very clear either. Have the Israelis engaged in a great crusade to save the Christians? I don't know when they became so deeply interested in the Christians. [Laughter.] But that's what they profess.

SENATOR JAVITS: I don't think that's an argument worthy of you, Senator Fulbright. The fact that they are anxious to save the Christians is to their credit, not to their debit. And I'm amazed, really, to hear you make that innuendo about people who want to save other people's lives. [Laughter. Applause.]

MR. FULBRIGHT: You're always amazed at anyone who disagrees with you.

MR. SISCO: Ladies and gentlemen, I regret that we have to cut this off at the moment, but there will be a further opportunity to discuss these issues, because we are about to take questions from the floor.

MR. SISCO: We have concluded the first segment of our program. I believe all of the panelists are in agreement that this year of 1977 is a year of opportunity. The panel is now open to questions from the experts in our audience and members of the press.

HASSAN YASSIN, director, Saudi Arabian Information Office in Washington: I would like to address this question to Mrs. Hauser who seems to know a great deal about the Israeli position. Do you believe that the Israeli government and people are reconciled to the idea of peace and a creation of a state of Palestine on the West Bank and in Gaza?

MRS. HAUSER: In my opinion, a large majority of the population are not reconciled to that proposition at this time, and for fairly sound security reasons. A Palestinian state on the

West Bank, without an elaborate security structure, would be very dangerous for Israel. It is evident why that would be the case in view of the weapons in the area. Such a state may come to pass after a period of normalization, in which the region becomes less hostile than it is today and the peaceful intentions of the parties become far more clear. An important ingredient in a peace conference is to get to that question after the other open questions of territory have been dealt with by the protagonist states. But, as of this time and place, a great number of Israelis would be extremely fearful about the creation of a Palestinian state, even if there were American guarantees of one kind or another.

Joseph J. Malone, president, Middle East Educational Trust, Inc.: A kind of garrison mentality comes through the paramilitary settlements such as those in Gush Etsion and Golan Heights. There have been seventy-seven settlements since 1967 beyond the green line. If there is an exponential factor in this, we will probably have 150 settlements in the ten years or so that Mrs. Hauser is talking about.

Many of my Israeli friends refer to their situation as having moved from one ghetto to a larger one. And there are two ways out of the ghetto, as I see it. One is expansion—what somebody once long ago called "perpetual war for perpetual peace"—and the other is conciliation, offering security both for Israelis and for Arabs. I would like to ask Senator Javits if he feels that this paramilitary redefining of borders represents a constructive approach.

Senator Javits: "Redefining of borders" and "paramilitary settlements" are your words, not mine, but I would like to deal with the settlement issue. It first arose at a security meeting in regard to areas contiguous to Israel. The Israelis' concept of their security involved more than having troops

23

there. That would not give them complete security. After all, they are in grave danger internally, as the surprise of the 1973 war proved. Israel sent its people to these settlements originally because of the security factor.

A large number of settlements—seventy odd—was mentioned and then extended in ten more years to 150. Nobody knows whether that is justified. If there is a peace agreement, a lot would probably be said about limiting the settlements or stopping them altogether, but there are only about 3,000 Israelis in all of the settlements, including the Golan Heights, compared with a population of roughly 800,000 to 900,000 in the West Bank. The settlements are not a matter of population transfers, but a matter of security, and the Israelis agree that the settlements are negotiable. There are several hundred thousand Arabs in Israel, and whatever becomes of the ultimate sovereignty of the West Bank, there will be 10,000, 20,000, or 50,000 Jews in Arab territory. There is nothing wrong with that, so long as it is understood that the fact of settlement does not imply sovereignty.

As I said in answer to Senator Fulbright, I am an advocate of the Israelis, but I thoroughly agree with our President and with the general wisdom that those settlements may or may not ultimately remain under Israeli jurisdiction. The fact that they are settled does not automatically confer Israeli jurisdiction, and they represent no threat to the effort to attain a peace.

EDWARD F. HENDERSON, former ambassador from Britain to Qatar: I served for a long time in the Arab world, and also in Israel and in Palestine. As a visitor to your lovely country, I have great admiration for many things here, especially the stand your President has taken on the question of human rights.

One thing perplexes me, and I hope the panel can make

me go away less disappointed than I might be otherwise. Why is the PLO singled out as the only group who cannot represent their own people? They are the representatives of Palestine, but they are not allowed to speak for them. And they are made to adhere to 242, but I do not see the same insistence that Israel should adhere to it, because they clearly flout it, utterly. I should like clarification, if I might, from the panel. Thank you.

MRS. HAUSER: I thought I commented on that during the first part of the program. The PLO has proven itself—in Lebanon in particular and certainly vis-à-vis Israel—to be an anarchic, destabilizing force which seeks to overturn the tranquillity of the area, not to speak of the safety and security of Israel.

The Rabat Conference accepted it as the representative of the Palestinian people without any referendum of the Palestinian people. That was shoved down the throat of King Hussein, who was not overjoyed at that prospect, since he would be a clear target of the PLO, as they made clear in the famous "Black October" when they tried to topple him.

Their interests are inimicable to our interests in the area, to the Saudi Arabian interests in the area, to the interests of the western world, which is a stable region, not susceptible to radicalization. The PLO is the avant-garde of Libya, of Iraq, of Algeria, of all the extreme, destabilizing forces in the area, and it serves no purpose for us to elevate them. I am puzzled why anyone would continue to do so when they are at their nadir, their lowest point in history, showing almost no ability to sustain themselves either on the battlefield or in the minds and hearts of the Palestinians. We would do well to try to push them down and out of the picture, rather than the opposite.

CHARLES F. SILLS, Middle East/Africa estimator, Department of Defense: Mrs. Hauser described Israel as a military asset, or ally, of the United States, and I would like her to clarify that. This interpretation appears somewhat different from the usual interpretation—that we have been transferring arms to Israel in order to promote a balance in the area, or to preserve some sort of American leverage in the situation.

MRS. HAUSER: For more than a decade, the Pentagon has continually pronounced publicly, at hearings in the Congress, that a strong Israel is our strongest defense against penetration by the Russians in the Mediterranean. That has been the underlying theory behind our military assistance to Israel. The fact that there is a democratic, stable, and strong Israel is certainly an impediment to Russian advancement in the area. I suppose the two senators here will have something to say about that subject. It has been the underlying argument, year in and year out, when military assistance has been debated in the Congress.

MR. FULBRIGHT: I would like to comment on that. I don't think that that is a fact of life. This is the theory the Israeli spokesmen for many years have promoted when they appear in Congress. But if it were not for Israel, the Russians never would have had any opportunity to make a foothold at all. The Arab countries—the major ones, at least—have never shown any disposition to be receptive to Soviet influence, except in their fear of the Israelis.

I don't think the Russians are threatening in any appreciable way, although the theory is that they are. General Brown did make a statement, as chairman of the joint chiefs, that there was quite a drain upon our military establishment in drawing off some of our best weapons to ship to Israel, some weapons that none of our NATO allies seem to have. But I don't think fear of the Russians is a sound reason for it.

JOYCE SHUB, legislative assistant for the Committee on Foreign Relations, Office of Senator Joseph Biden (Democrat, Delaware): I would like to know if there is any general agreement, in principle, among the panel members that a homeland for the Palestinians would be necessary for a permanent peace. And if so, which area or which country would be both satisfactory to the Palestinians and least threatening to the Israelis?

SENATOR JAVITS: I have debated the issue of homeland for the Palestinians very sharply. The President himself has abandoned that idea. He has now spoken of an entity rather than a homeland.

The question presupposes the lack of a homeland, or the absence of an area which is secure and able to be settled by Palestinian Arabs. But the fact is that hundreds of thousands have been dispersed throughout the Arab world. The Arab world is enormous, with a huge population: Jordan is a country in which there are several hundred thousand Palestinian Arabs. The only barrier is their tenacious clinging to the refugee camps on the political theory that they will be a platform for the conquest of Israel.

We have supported those refugee camps, through UNRRA. I have backed that support because I don't want confrontation for any reason, even if the reason is a good one. I don't think a confrontation would be helpful to the situation in the area.

For what and for whom is the Palestinian homeland idea proposed? If these people were homeless and incapable of being settled anywhere, like the Jews, then there would be a reason for proposing a homeland, especially if they had suffered the holocaust and the persecution of Hitler. But the Palestinian homeland simply reflects a desire to have a political state in which the PLO chieftains can be the principal officials. As Mrs. Hauser has pointed out, and as I have pointed out, they have not shown any right to be trusted with that kind of power.

Let us not forget that Israel can be cut in two in the twinkling of an eye, if the PLO establishes its state within the territory of the West Bank. If eight to twelve miles of Israel are taken, it is cut in two. Maybe my colleagues will argue that shells can be dropped on the Israelis now. But the history of war, including war in the Middle East, indicates that fatal damage must be inflicted on the ground.

The Israelis have a right to be mortally afraid of that, especially from the PLO, which has caused such anarchy and havoc in Lebanon. And let's not forget that. That isn't Arafat being a moderate. That is death and destruction every day for months on end, unremitting and unforgiving. And that is what the Israelis would have to look forward to, and that has to be understood.

Mr. BALL: One cannot escape the fact that there are something like 1,100,000 Arabs in the West Bank and the Gaza Strip. If we give them an area in which they can exercise the right of self-determination—which seems to be quite fundamental in the American credo and which, I suppose, is one of the things that human rights is all about—then I suppose that we would have to give them a chance to stay there.

There are 3,000 Israelis in the West Bank, as against 1,100,000 Arabs, as the senator pointed out. I cannot envisage a transfer of population to some place else, so the question is, How do they obtain the right of self-determination in the West Bank and the Gaza Strip? All the indications are that if the people were permitted to exercise self-determination, they would choose the PLO as their representatives. This has certainly been what the local elections have suggested. Recent local elections have been overwhelmingly on the PLO side.

We are not talking about people who should not have a right to a homeland. They are there. There are 1,100,000 of them there, and I don't know how they might be disposed. Certainly, to let them stay under military occupation, as they have been for a decade, seems to me to be quite contrary to all the principles this country has represented.

MOUMMED SHADID, visiting professor at Georgetown University: First of all, I would like to comment on the projection of the Palestinian position in Lebanon as some sort of a Muslim holocaust against the Christians. Actually 30 percent of the Palestinian people are Christians, so I think that this is an anomaly and an attempt to project an image of the Palestinians that is not precise.

I would like to ask all the distinguished panelists whether—in the history of negotiations between contending parties—any party has a right to dictate the negotiating part of the others? Does the Israeli government have a right to dictate who constitutes Palestinian representation when the United Nations, the Arab League, the Nonaligned Conference, and 98 percent of the states in the world recognize the PLO as the representative of the Palestinian people?

MRS. HAUSER: I think there's a fairly simple answer to that in international law. I know of no conference for the determination of peace after a conflict in modern history in which anything other than states was represented. In the Versailles Conference, when the states of Europe gathered to make the peace, the Ottoman and Austro-Hungarian empires were dismembered, and peoples of all kinds who had no statehood were displaced. When their time came, they were heard on whether or not they would have a state, and whether they would stay where they were or be removed to other places. In the wisdom, or lack of wisdom, of the governing states, various decisions were made at Versailles.

That is the way to approach this Geneva conference. There can be Palestinians in the Jordanian delegation, in the Syrian delegation, and in the Lebanese delegation, certainly. When the issue of displaced refugees is reached on the conference agenda, then the PLO has a right to be heard, along with any other representatives of the refugees that may be in existence at the time. But to open the conference by elevating the PLO to some sort of delegation status is to predetermine the outcome. It would have already been decided that the PLO is entitled to be treated as a state and presumably would be awarded with statehood.

That is anomalous. I know of no other event in international peace conferences like that.

BEN J. WATTENBERG, senior fellow, American Enterprise Institute: In the present discussion, I am a pro-Christian and a pro-Israeli. My question is addressed to Senator Fulbright. I wonder why it is, sir, that you and Secretary Ball, and the representatives of the Arab states, were not in favor of a Palestinian state for the almost twenty years when the West Bank was under Arab control?

MR. FULBRIGHT: I don't recall that that became an issue at that time of any real consequence. [Laughter.]

MR. WATTENBERG: Why not?

MR. FULBRIGHT: Well, the West Bank was then part of Jordan, up until 1967, as I recall.

MR. WATTENBERG: Should it perhaps belong there again?

MR. FULBRIGHT: I would have no objection to it. This is a decision that President Sadat of Egypt and others have said would be acceptable. I don't think that the other Arab states would object to it. The principle has been to allow the Palestinians self-determination, as Mr. Ball has said. If they felt it was useful to affiliate with Jordan, I doubt if anyone would object to that.

MR. BALL: There was a time when the prime minister of Israel asked me why we were interested in King Hussein and in promoting the peace with the Jordanians; the Israelis did not care whether Hussein lived or died. They were totally indifferent to him.

At that time the Israelis were not prepared to undertake serious talks with Jordan, and indeed Hussein was under some constraints himself because of his fear of Nasser. What was at issue at that time was the problem of an agreement with Jordan involving the Arabs in the West Bank and Gaza Strip. There was no disinclination to deal with that issue then. It was simply that the physical facts were different. Before 1967, Hussein was in control of the situation.

MRS. HAUSER: But the taking over the West Bank by Jordan in 1950 was unlawful, and it is recognized to this day only by Great Britain and Pakistan. None of the Arab world has ever recognized that annexation. Neither has Israel; neither has the United States. Our view officially, as a matter of law, was that Jordan was a military occupier of the West Bank, which was seized in the 1948-1949 war, and that its annexation was illegal. That is also the position of Egypt; that is the position of Syria; that is the position of Saudi Arabia.

MR. BALL: You are making an argument in favor of self-determination for the Palestinians, which is exactly the point I am trying to make. And the West Bank might not necessarily end up in Jordan.

31

SENATOR JAVITS: On this issue of self-determination for the Palestinians, the Arab world at Rabat a few years ago turned the West Bank over to the PLO. They did not consult the people there. They did not allow Hussein to make a case to those people. They ruled out the people.

And now there is an effort to rule them out again, indeed to rule out any alternative but the PLO, because it is in place and it is very militant. The attitude of the Arab world is to give in to them and avoid a lot of trouble. The Arab world has yet to reverse the position it took at Rabat and give the people of the West Bank an opportunity to consider other alternatives for themselves—such as becoming an independent state or forming a union with Jordan. And, if you gentlemen on the panel are right, we do not propose to give them that opportunity. Instead, we will let them be taken over by 30,000 PLO riflemen, who will probably liquidate all the mayors the people elected.

MR. BALL: Let's be a little calmer about it, senator. In the first place, the Arab states have gone back to some extent from the action that was taken at Rabat. But in any event—

SENATOR JAVITS: They have not done a thing about it. Show me where and when they have drawn back. I am all in favor of trying to get an act of self-determination by the PLO as a part of a peace conference, and if it could be supervised by the UN or by some objective party of that kind, why, that would be fine. I am no advocate for the PLO, but I do think it is rather extraordinary to suggest that having one or two PLO leaders in other Arab delegations somehow prejudices the whole situation. Certainly, it does not prejudice the situation any more than having Israeli settlements in Palestine territory does. These matters are subject to determination by the peace agreement itself.

RUSSELL WARREN HOWE, Washington correspondent, *Saturday Review Magazine*: I would like to ask a question of Mr. Ball, and anyone else on the panel who wishes to reply. If the present Israeli government's policy of expanding settlements in the occupied territory should lead to another war, and if the Arab countries made it clear, as they more or less did in 1973, that their objective was purely the implementation of Resolution 242, and not an attack on Israeli territory itself, what should be the policy of the United States, in particular in regard to military resupply to Israel?

MR. BALL: It is very hard to make a decision now about a contingency which, if it arises, is not likely to arise in the exact way you mention.

I am not very concerned about whether the Israeli settlements in Palestine are legal or not. I am concerned about them for only one reason: they reinforce the Arab fear of Israeli expansionism. When that fear is coupled with Mr. Begin's statements about the Israeli right to the territory as part of the Promised Land, the Arabs remember as well as anyone else that the Promised Land included part of Jordan, too. And a question arises as to just what is the Israeli long-range intention.

I think that my Israeli friends have no expansionist ideas in mind at all. I think they would love to reach an agreement, and I think they are honestly and sincerely working towards that goal. But I do think that the symbolism of those Israeli settlements plays on an underlying phobia, an underlying fear that everyone is neurotic in this area, on both sides. We ought to try not to exacerbate the pervasive paranoia of this situation, and that is what the settlements do.

MR. FULBRIGHT: I want to underline that. That is exactly it. We are concerned not over settlements, as such, but over the intention. What are the long-term intentions of the Israeli government? That is also true with regard to the PLO or the Palestinians.

I don't understand why there isn't more sympathy for the lot of Palestinians. They have really had a very rough go. I don't know anyone qualified to judge whether or not the PLO is the proper representative, but it has been designated by the people and by the Arab countries. I don't agree at all with Senator Javits that the only purpose of the PLO is to have 30,000 rifles to kill all of the Israelis down there. I don't think that is their purpose at all. I think the Palestinians have a legitimate feeling about that territory, like other people who have been ousted from their homes, wherever they may be, in any part of the world. And I think we should be more sympathetic to it.

SENATOR JAVITS: May I just complete that thought by saying I hope and pray that the peace conference does find a self-determination solution which is not prejudiced and which gives the people an opportunity to develop their own consciousness, their own politics, in their own way.

MR. FULBRIGHT: But we will never know it unless we have a conference.

SENATOR JAVITS: We are going to have a conference, Senator Fulbright. I am not a prophet of doom in this. On the contrary, I see hope. We are going to have a conference.

MR. FULBRIGHT: You are well informed, and I hope you are right. The newspapers are a little gloomy these days.

MR. SISCO: I think it would be appropriate for me to ask, at this point, how much flexibility each side has, assuming we do get a negotiation, as I think everyone here in this audience hopes for.

We have alluded to the wide gap on the substance of an overall settlement between the two sides. We have very delicate domestic situations in the Arab world, and there is a very dynamic political process in Israel. How much flexibility will we find on each side once we get to Geneva?

SENATOR JAVITS: My own opinion is that we are dealing here in time, more than in space. In other words, this situation should have an opportunity to stabilize. Discussing it here, we pick up an argument on this item or that item, because in a sense we are deeply involved and partisan. But when what the panel feels is totaled up, I believe that negotiations will be shown to be possible, given an opportunity in time, and given the negotiating framework which I now see developing. But if we try to prepackage the outcome and put the PLO in because of what happened at Rabat, we will not get anywhere.

The way to approach it is to get the parties to Geneva with a commitment from all of them that Israel is a nation and will remain so, as the United Nations already determined under Resolution 242.

If that basis is laid, then, given the necessary time within which this thing can develop, peace can be negotiated.

Mind you, we should not let the time drift by. The agreement has to indicate the exact stages and phases of what will take place. We cannot have an open-ended proposition that will take years to negotiate. But the people on the West Bank and the people of Israel must have an opportunity to become accustomed to the new situation they will both face within the time agreed upon, when they have to make their decisions.

MR. FULBRIGHT: I agree with this. The agreement in principle on the ultimate solution, even though it takes time, is what is important.

Mrs. Hauser: I think the conference contemplates breaking up immediately into working groups, between the Israelis and the Egyptians, the Israelis and the Jordanians, the Israelis and the Syrians. Then there will be pushing and pulling and tugging on those Arab countries more amenable to settlement. The Egyptians are the most readily disposed at the moment to go forward. That is the only way the conference would work successfully, and that is what the American approach contemplates.

Mr. Sisco: I do see a general consensus on this point—once we get to the conference, there will be sufficient give and take to make it a very hopeful thing indeed. I am very pleased to hear that.

Mr. Ball: Qualify that.

Mr. Sisco: I spoke too soon.

Mr. Ball: You asked how much flexibility there was on each side. My answer was the one that I have given before—the United States has to help each side make the decision, and the United States has to take the blame for the decision. Otherwise the two sides will not make the decision, because they are prisoners of their own domestic politics. Each side can only go a certain way down the road. We have to appear to bring pressure, so they can say they really do not want to do this but the Americans are making them do it. And that will bring about a settlement. We will not get one otherwise.

Senator Javits: If the word *pressure* were left out, I could agree with that. The United States has enough weight in the situation. We all know that. The Israelis know it, and the Arabs know it. But the minute the word *pressure* is used, everybody's back is up, unnecessarily.

MR. FULBRIGHT: I wouldn't use the word. I would just do it.

MARGARET C. BROWN, staff member, Senate Foreign Relations Committee: There is one thing that puzzles me. What do we do about the Golan Heights? If the Arabs possess them, they threaten the Israelis. If the Israelis possess them, they threaten the Arabs. These peace conferences are very lovely, but what about that little detail?

MRS. HAUSER: The Golan Heights is not a difficult question to resolve. Buffer zones would be contemplated for a substantial period of time—demilitarization and eventual withdrawal from the heights by the Israelis in various stages. That is not a very terribly complex problem for the conference.

MS. BROWN: Would no one be there?

MRS. HAUSER: There would eventually be a repeopling of the heights, as this buffer zone is moved out. But that would come over a fairly lengthy period of time.

ED ROSENBAUM, Middle East Studies Association: I wanted to ask a question directly about the issue of compromise, especially toward the PLO. The history of the Palestinian-Arab nationalist movement has shown that, at various crucial times in the past, the PLO or its ancestor organizations have been unwilling to compromise, particularly at points at which compromise might have been advantageous to them. I would like to ask the members of the panel why they believe that the upcoming Geneva conference, if it does

37

happen, will be an opportunity for them to change this pattern of theirs?

MR. FULBRIGHT: Yesterday, I watched Barbara Walters's television interview with Mr. Arafat. She asked if he would accept the West Bank for the Palestinians and, I think, Gaza. If I understood him correctly, he said he would. She emphasized very strongly it was the first time in public he had ever said that. It was a very brief interview, because part of the tapes were destroyed. But she interpreted it to mean that he would accept it, and she left the impression that he means he would accept it, and cease the war and the terrorism.

MR. BALL: The real hope for a flexible, moderate, sensible Arab position will come from the major Arab front-line states, particularly the Saudi Arabians. Because they control the money supply of the area, they are in a very strong position to bring about a moderate, general Arab attitude. This is what will happen as far as the PLO is concerned.

I would leave it to the Saudis, the Syrians, and the others to take care of the PLO. They will do it in time, because they do not want an irresponsible Arab state in control. That is the last thing in the world they want.

MR. FULBRIGHT: As a footnote to that, if we can ever reach an agreement—even though it takes time, as Senator Javits said—people like the Saudis are so concerned about radicalization and trouble that they would be most forthcoming in trying to calm it down in all areas there. They do have the means, and their first priority is peace in the area. I agree with what you said.

SENATOR JAVITS: That is why I expressed optimism here, because I do believe that the forces in the Arab world and in the Israeli world are developing toward that end. I don't agree with the conclusion that Mr. Begin will do nothing and that he is uncompromising, or that he has the conquest of Samaria or Judea or Jordan on his mind.

MR. FULBRIGHT: Well, he gives that impression.

SENATOR JAVITS: Well, maybe he is a very good negotiator and deliberately gives that impression. But, in my judgment, the exigencies are such that once the parties get going on the peace process, the ideas we have been discussing will develop. The PLO may or may not be involved. One of the difficulties with our debate is that we assume the PLO has to represent the Palestinian people.

MR. FULBRIGHT: That is right.

SENATOR JAVITS: They may choose the PLO to speak for them, if given a chance. If they do, we may all have to live with the PLO. But they may not, and the Israelis are entitled to have the benefit of the opportunity. Maybe they can be much more convincing than the PLO, or maybe Hussein can be. Maybe the Palestinians themselves will develop a mayor or a set of mayors they would prefer. Give them a chance. Give them the opportunity. Don't foreclose it with the Rabat dictate, which says the PLO is the only legitimate representative of the Palestinian people.

EMILE NAKHLEH, professor of political science, Mount St. Mary's College: I just returned from the West Bank, and since the issue of representation has figured in this discussion, I would like to ask Mrs. Hauser to explain her strong rejection of the PLO as a representative of the Palestinians in the light of the following five facts: (1) Last year's election in the West Bank indicated a strong support for the PLO. (2) Israel has so far failed in developing any new leadership on the West Bank, other than the PLO. (3) Every academic study done by the Hebrew University and the University of Haifa indicated that a majority of the West Bank Arabs regard the PLO as their representative. (4) Every study conducted among Palestinian Arabs in Israel itself indicated that the majority view the PLO as their representative. (5) The most recent statement by West Bank mayors, especially those in Nablus, Ramla, and Hebron, indicated that the PLO is their representative.

MRS. HAUSER: I think we have answered that throughout the course of this discussion. There has never been a free and open plebiscite among Palestinians on the West Bank and elsewhere on who their representative should be.

The decision at Rabat was taken at the insistence of the more radical Arab countries, and King Hussein was most unhappy with it. He has not quite accustomed himself to it, and he seeks every opportunity to evade it, as do some of the other Arab countries.

What is important is that the conference unfold without prejudging that question. If we ask the PLO to the conference as a representative of the Palestinian people, we will have prejudged the most difficult question to be faced by the peace conference. I feel confident in saying Israel will not accept that prejudgment. I would like to believe that our own government will not urge that solution upon Israel under any circumstances.

If the PLO would like to accommodate the world and renounce its covenant, to destroy Israel, which it refused to do very recently, maybe the world would take a very different attitude toward it. But the PLO has reiterated its destructive intention on every occasion thus far.

Why our country should be in the position of elevating that organization escapes me. As I said earlier, the PLO is in its lowest state in the last decade. It has been virtually used out in the battle in Lebanon, and if the struggle there continues very much longer, it is my opinion it will be totally used out. I see no merit—factually, legally, morally—in pushing the PLO to the center point, which will only serve to derail the Geneva conference.

MR. SISCO: A number of members this evening have alluded indirectly to the Soviet role in the Middle East. How do the panelists view the Soviet role at a renewed Geneva conference, and in this whole peace process?

MR. BALL: It is impossible to be very categorical about it. If they are given a role to play in making peace, they would rather see peace in the area than take the great risk of further turbulence.

MR. FULBRIGHT: I agree with that. It was just a few years ago that Gromyko publicly stated that the U.S.S.R. would enter into a joint guarantee of the area, and they have given every indication they would do that.

SENATOR JAVITS: My own judgment is that the Soviet Union enjoys targets of opportunity. The vindication of U.S. policy is that we are the principal factor in the Middle East, and I hope we remain so. Considering the Soviet Union's backing of Libya, of Iraq, and of the PLO, I would be very worried that it will again choose, as it has in Africa and in many other places, to fish in troubled waters. I hope that the situation remains as it is, that the United States uses its paramount position so intelligently that the Soviet Union is necessarily satisfied with an accompanying role.

LARRY MOSHER, writer in residence, Georgetown University: I would like to ask Mrs. Hauser this question concerning Palestinian representation. The debate seems to have

41

edged around the problem of perception—psychological perceptions and fears. Most of the panel has agreed that Israeli fears have been or should be taken into consideration when Israel is asked to deal with the PLO. What about the Palestinian fears of not being represented at all, in any peace agreement? What guarantees to them that a plebiscite, that some determination of their own choosing, could be hammered out?

MRS. HAUSER: The Palestinians certainly ought to press their spokesmen, which are the Arab countries, to make certain that that question is on the agenda of the conference. It logically would be, in any event.

As I said before, there should be Palestinians in the delegations of Jordan, Lebanon, and Syria, where they reside. That is perfectly proper, and I assume the Israelis would have no objection. In fact, they have said they would have no objection to a delegation so composed. That is the proper way to approach an international conference. When the broader question of displaced Palestinians comes up—what I like to call the refugee problem—then, as I said earlier, it is perfectly proper for all kinds of spokesmen for the refugees to be heard, in order that a final decision can be made as to their fate.

MR. SISCO: Ladies and gentlemen, this concludes another public policy forum presented by the American Enterprise Institute for Public Policy Research. On behalf of AEI, I wish to thank our distinguished panelists, Senator Javits, Mr. Fulbright, Mr. Ball, and Mrs. Hauser, and also the experts and members of the press and our guests here this evening who have participated so actively. [Applause.]